TORNADOES

MICHAEL WOODS AND MARY B. WOODS

To Dominic Calarco and Mary Vizzeri, Joseph Gullo and Martha Patti, Edward Boulle and Margaret Marshall, James Boyle and Catherine Golden

Editor's note: Determining the exact death toll following disasters is often difficult—if not impossible—especially in the case of disasters that took place long ago. The authors and the editors in this series have used their best judgment in determining which figures to include.

Lerner Publications Company
A division of Lerner Publishing Group
241 First Avenue North
Minneapolis, MN 55401 U.S.A.

Website address: www.lernerbooks.com

Library of Congress Cataloging-in-Publication Data

Woods, Michael, 1946–
    Tornadoes / by Michael Woods and Mary B. Woods.
      p.   cm. -- (Disasters up close)
    Includes bibliographical references and index.
    ISBN-13: 978–0–8225–4714–3 (lib. bdg. : alk. paper)
    ISBN-10: 0–8225–4714–7 (lib. bdg. : alk. paper)
    1. Tornadoes—Juvenile literature. I. Woods, Mary B. (Mary Boyle), 1946–
II. Title. III. Series: Woods, Michael, 1946– Disasters up close.
QC955.2.W66 2007
551.55'3—dc22   2005017134

Manufactured in the United States of America
1 2 3 4 5 6 – DP – 12 11 10 09 08 07

Contents

Introduction

"We had a terrible wind all day long," said firefighter Matt Timmel of Newburgh, Indiana. "It just started increasing and increasing."

That "terrible wind" grew into a tornado—a swirling cone of wind and dust that swept across Kentucky and southern Indiana on November 6, 2005. The tornado did the most damage in Indiana, where it struck at about 2 A.M. Its raging winds caught most people asleep and off guard. Paul Adams remembered that he was sleeping when "all of a sudden . . . the whole building shook, our window broke, and there was water pouring in." Paul's roommate Tyler Moss said that "it sounded like there was a jet engine in our apartment."

Tornadoes, which are also called twisters, sweep up all sorts of material, called debris. That debris can include everything from stones and glass to trucks and cows. When the storm had passed, it left behind splintered trees, wrecked homes, and smashed cars. Chad Bennett, a Newburgh firefighter, described "a whole apartment complex that lost all of the top floors of the units." And Newburgh resident Sherri Hudson saw her whole house ripped apart. She and her husband were lucky enough to reach their basement safely. But, she said, "we no sooner got down there than it was like a bomb exploded. All the debris came falling down the stair," she said in an interview. "The only thing left are the cabinets in my kitchen. The dishes are still in them untouched."

The storm killed 24 people, injured at least 200 more, and destroyed more than 500 homes. It was Indiana's deadliest tornado in more than 30 years.

A trailer frame was stuck atop a tree trunk after a tornado tore through Alberta, Canada, in July 2000.

AWESOME DISASTERS

Tornadoes are some of nature's most amazing and powerful storms. Winds rush as fast as 300 miles per hour (483 kilometers per hour). Twisters arrive with a roar that many people compare to the sound of a freight train. And the strongest storms can lift real train cars weighing more than 50 tons (45 metric tons) and throw them onto their sides.

Hundreds of tornadoes strike every year. Yet scientists still don't understand them completely. And in the past, twisters were often complete surprises. People did not have weather forecasts (predictions) to tell them that a storm was coming. Modern weather forecasting equipment can often give people advance warning of a tornado, giving them more time to find shelter. Nevertheless, twisters can still be terrible disasters that cause great destruction. When more than 50 tornadoes ripped through the midwest and south in April 2006, more than 1,200 buildings were destroyed. Many people lost everything—and 27 lost their lives.

Residents of Evansville, Indiana, work to clean up their home after the powerful November 2005 twister tore apart their home.

" *When I woke up, [it] sounded like hail hitting the window and all of a sudden the whole house just exploded.* "

—Casey Lockhart, describing the November 2005 tornado that hit his rural Indiana home

Terrible Tornadoes

TORNADOES ARE AMONG THE WORLD'S SMALLEST YET MOST VIOLENT STORMS. THEY ARE FUNNEL-SHAPED AREAS OF AIR THAT SPIN VERY FAST. WINDS IN SOME TORNADOES SWIRL AT MORE THAN 300 MILES PER HOUR (483 KM/HR). THAT'S FIVE TIMES AS FAST AS A CAR ON THE HIGHWAY.

People sometimes call tornadoes twisters. These spiral-shaped clouds do twist through the air. Twisters form in certain kinds of thunderstorms. In fact, the word *tornado* comes from the Spanish word *tronada*, which means "thunderstorm."

"It looked like a big cloud of wind coming," said Shirley Reale, a retired school secretary. In 2004 a twister hit her home in Campbelltown, Pennsylvania. "Stuff was flying everywhere."

OFF TO MUNCHKINLAND?

Tornadoes don't always hit the ground. Sometimes they blow along many feet above the land. If a tornado does touch the ground, the spinning wind can cause great damage. And tornadoes don't stay in one place. They move across the ground, damaging everything in their path. A tornado may stay on the ground for seconds or hours.

A tornado's winds push and tear at buildings and other structures. Powerful twisters can rip apart houses, schools, and stores. They can tear down trees, electric power lines, and telephone lines. The wind scatters heavy objects almost like a fan blowing a stack of paper across a tabletop.

MINI-CYCLONES

Tornadoes are the smallest kind of cyclones, storms with wind that spins in a circle. Most twisters are about as wide as several football fields end to end. Hurricanes and typhoons are the biggest cyclones. They often are the width of a state.

A tornado touched down in Aken, Germany, in June 2004. The tornado partially destroyed nearly 100 buildings in the small town.

Strong tornadoes can't carry people to other worlds, as the tornado in *The Wizard of Oz* did to Dorothy. But they can pick up people, cows, cars, trucks, and even mobile homes. The whirling wind can make these objects sail through the air and fall down far away. One tornado picked up a motel sign in Broken Bow, Oklahoma, and dropped it 30 miles (48 km) away in Arkansas.

The famous tornado scene from the 1939 movie *The Wizard of Oz* carries Dorothy's house (below) to Oz.

SUCKED UP

Dorothy and her little dog, Toto, got sucked up into a tornado in *The Wonderful Wizard of Oz*, a book by L. Frank Baum. In real life, many things do get caught in tornadoes—including people, sometimes. But tornadoes usually don't hurt people by lifting them high into the sky. Instead, most tornado injuries and deaths occur when people are thrown to the side by wind or are hit by debris.

D IS FOR DAMAGE

Wind causes most tornado damage. Lightning and hail from thunderstorms that form tornadoes can add to the damage. The severe thunderstorms that come before tornadoes may produce hail the size of golf balls. These chunks of ice can smash windows, dent the metal on cars, and destroy farmers' crops.

Don E. Halsey took pictures of the damage in Xenia, Ohio, after a tornado struck in 1974. "The picture that amazed me the most was of an automobile rolled up into a near perfect ball," he said. Someone had driven the car right into the tornado.

Life imitates art: a 1950 Texas tornado carried this house 75 feet (23 meters) before setting it down on its side.

Two residents of Brandenburg, Kentucky, pick through debris after the 1974 tornado destroyed half the town.

> " The next thing I saw
> was a scene I shall never forget. . . .
> destruction you read about
> that happens to other places,
> but never to your own. "
>
> —John J. Scott, describing Brandenburg, Kentucky,
> after a 1974 tornado

Tornadoes in towns and cities can cause terrible disasters because many people and buildings are close together. These whirlwinds cause billions of dollars in damage in the United States each year. Tornadoes kill about 70 people every year and seriously injure about 1,500 others.

In early May 2003, tornadoes caused more than 40 deaths during a single week. Almost four hundred tornadoes broke out in Oklahoma and more than a dozen other U.S. states during that week. That's more than in any other week in U.S. history.

David Waller had a close call with one of those twisters. He was driving an eighteen-wheel tractor-trailer truck on Interstate 40 near Oklahoma City, Oklahoma, on May 8, 2003. Suddenly, in the distance, he saw a tornado coming right toward him. Waller pulled to the side of the road and jumped into a ditch to take shelter. Then the fierce storm picked up his truck and dropped it on one side. He later remembered being "scared to death."

Several days earlier, weather forecasters had seen that conditions were perfect for a tornado outbreak. They issued warnings as twisters approached. These warnings gave many people time to take shelter from the twisters. But they could not save everyone or everything. In that one terrible week, hundreds of people were injured and thousands of homes and businesses were badly damaged. The cost of the destruction totaled hundreds of millions of dollars.

THE GREAT NATCHEZ TORNADO

One of the worst tornadoes in history hit the Mississippi town of Natchez on May 7, 1840. History books say that it killed 317 people. However, the real number of deaths may have been much higher. At that time, people in the southern United States owned slaves. Officials didn't bother to count slaves who died on plantations (large farms) because slaves were considered property. We may never know how many slaves died in the Great Natchez Tornado.

A twister approaches a house in Kansas in 2004. The National Weather Service recorded 1,717 tornados in the United States that year, an all-time record.

1880 MARSHFIELD TORNADO

A damaged street in Marshfield, Missouri

An eight-year-old boy named W. D. Chitty was the weather forecaster for the great Marshfield, Missouri, tornado. On April 18, 1880, Chitty looked out the window. He saw what looked like a cone-shaped column of smoke billowing into the air near a neighbor's house.

"I grabbed my father's knee and said, 'Look. Cohen's house is on fire.' . . . My father looked steadily for a moment and then leaped to his feet with a cry, 'My God, it's a tornado!' " Chitty and his family ran to take shelter in the town courthouse, one of the sturdiest buildings in town. *"The square was filled with excited people running in all directions and looking and pointing at the approaching funnel-like cloud,"* he remembered. *"The wind had*

Dust and debris hang in the air over the ruins of Marshfield.

"*The wind... rose to a fiendish shriek.*"
—W. D. Chitty

risen so rapidly that in the few seconds it took to get across the courthouse yard, my father had to pull my mother by main strength to get her into the lobby."

After the wind stopped, nobody dared to leave the shelter for a few minutes. When they did, people saw a wrecked town. The Chittys' house was in a block of strong brick buildings. The tornado, however, ripped off the second story of the buildings like a giant swinging an axe. *"We instinctively moved toward the direction of what had been our home, but what was now nothing but a barren floor with a few remnants of shattered walls and rubbish,"* Chitty said.

This massive twister was one of the twenty-five most deadly tornado disasters in U.S. history. It killed about 90 people—almost one out of every ten people in Marshfield—and injured about 200 more. And it damaged nearly every building in town. Chitty's family and dozens of others lost their homes.

Musician John W. Boone honored the Marshfield disaster and its victims in song. His piano tune "Marshfield Tornado" sounded like the rush and roar of a tornado. The twister tune, however, was disastrous for the piano. When Boone tried to record it, he played so loudly and the song had so many notes that the piano broke.

What Causes Tornadoes?

PEOPLE IN KANSAS, MISSOURI, AND SIX OTHER STATES WERE ENJOYING A PLEASANT SPRING DAY ON MAY 4, 2003. BUT TWO AIR MASSES WERE ABOUT TO SEND THEM RUNNING FOR SHELTER. AN AIR MASS IS A LARGE BODY OF AIR. DIFFERENT AIR MASSES HAVE DIFFERENT TEMPERATURES AND MOISTURE LEVELS. THEY CAN BE WARM OR COLD AND DRY OR MOIST. WHEN THEY MEET, TORNADOES FORM.

One mass of cold, dry air moved southward from the Rocky Mountains. Another mass of warm, moist air came northward from the Gulf of Mexico. When the two air masses mixed together, 94 tornadoes formed in eight states. The twisters killed 38 people and caused more than $150 million in damage.

"The atmosphere created a perfect set up for a . . . spring severe weather outbreak," said Dan McCarthy, a meteorologist. Meteorologists report and forecast the weather. They also study conditions in the atmosphere that cause storms and other kinds of weather. The atmosphere is the layer of air above Earth's surface.

THE NO-NO WORD

Until 1952 weather forecasters in the United States could not use the word *tornado* in forecasts. Government officials banned the word because tornado forecasts were not accurate. They worried that a prediction could do even more harm than a tornado. It might make people panic. They could get hurt trying to escape. The ban ended after tornado forecasting improved in the late 1940s.

Kansas meteorology students monitor a storm for tornado-related activity.

Trees were broken in half by a tornado that swept through China in June 2005.

INGREDIENTS IN THE RECIPE

Most tornadoes form in severe thunderstorms called supercells. Not all bad thunderstorms produce tornadoes. Meteorologists don't know exactly why some thunderstorms produce deadly twisters and others don't. But they have learned a lot about supercells.

For supercells to form, the atmosphere must have certain ingredients. First, the air must have enough moisture to feed the storm. That moisture comes from water vapor, which is liquid water that has evaporated and changed into an invisible gas. Water vapor makes the air feel humid. Tornadoes also need a layer of warm air near the ground, with a layer of cold air above it.

These conditions occur when cold air masses plow into warm masses of air. As the different air masses meet, they form a boundary called a weather front. Along the front, the warm, moist air rises in currents called updrafts. The warm air grows cooler as it rises. As it cools, the water vapor in the air condenses, or changes back to a liquid. Those tiny drops of water form towering thunderclouds.

An anvil cloud (a flat-topped cloud that makes up part of a thunderstorm) at sunset

The change from a gas to a liquid releases heat. Heat helps the air continue rising, until it reaches heights of 30,000 feet (9,144 m) or more. At about that level, the air stops rising. It spreads sideways to form a flat-topped thunderstorm cloud.

This Monticello, Indiana, high school was flattened by a killer tornado in 1974.

PUTTING THE TWIST IN TWISTERS

The next step in making a twister is for the rising air to start spinning. Something called wind shear makes this happen. Wind shear occurs when winds at different heights move in different directions, different speeds, or both. Wind shear produces a wide, horizontal tube of rapidly spinning air.

Sometimes, as updrafts continue rising and downdrafts blow toward the earth, they push on the spinning tube of air until it stands on end. This upright column of wind is called a mesocyclone. The mesocyclone is the part of the storm that actually produces tornadoes. It spins faster and faster through the supercell. Nearby clouds spin along with it, sometimes dropping a little lower in a huge wall cloud. This massive cloud formation looks like a dark wall of clouds hanging in the sky. Sometimes the wall cloud itself will spin for thirty minutes or so and then disappear. But at other times, it will produce a tornado that drops down out of the cloud.

A mesocyclone and wall cloud may form one tornado or several at the same time. However, only about half of mesocyclones produce tornadoes. Some mesocyclones run out of the warm, moist air that releases heat and keeps updrafts going. They dry up and fizzle out.

A TWISTER IN YOUR TUB

Fill up a bathtub or sink, and watch water run down the drain *(above)*. You'll see a little whirlpool that forms at the drain. This whirlpool is called a vortex. A vortex is water or air that spins. A tornado is a vortex of air.

A mesocyclone created this tornado, which struck Oklahoma in May 1999.

TWISTER TOTALS

Millions of thunderstorms occur each year. Fortunately, only rare storms produce tornadoes. In an average year, 800 to 1,200 tornadoes are reported in the United States. More twisters probably strike in remote areas where nobody notices or reports them.

Tornadoes can form one at a time. In addition, several may form together in outbreaks. These outbreaks can cause great disasters. On May 3, 1999, at least fifty-nine tornadoes touched down in central Oklahoma. They killed forty-one people, destroyed hundreds of homes and other buildings, and caused $1.2 billion in damage.

FUN FACT

A tornado's strong winds can carry small objects for great distances. In 1915 a bank check may have taken the longest journey. The Great Bend Tornado carried the check more than 200 miles (322 km), taking it from Kansas to neighboring Nebraska.

Sometimes tornadoes occur shortly after a hurricane. The Louisiana town below was hit by such a tornado after Hurricane Andrew in 1992.

THE FORMATION OF A TORNADO

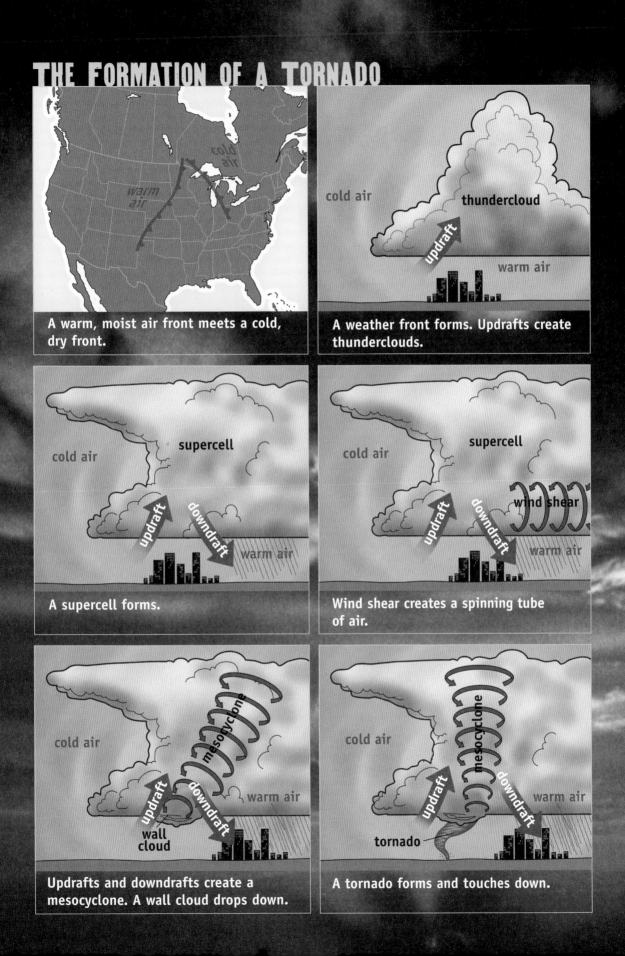

A warm, moist air front meets a cold, dry front.

A weather front forms. Updrafts create thunderclouds.

A supercell forms.

Wind shear creates a spinning tube of air.

Updrafts and downdrafts create a mesocyclone. A wall cloud drops down.

A tornado forms and touches down.

1925 TRI-STATE TORNADO

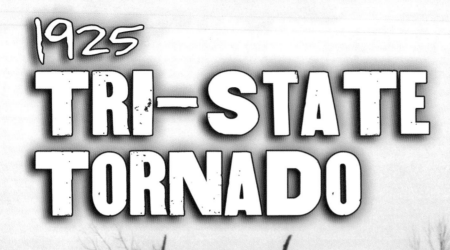

A group of men surveyed the damage in Griffin, Indiana.

Weather experts predicted strong shifting winds for eastern Missouri, southern Illinois, and southwestern Indiana for March 18, 1925. Nobody dreamed how forcefully the wind would actually blow.

At 1:01 P.M., a tornado touched down in Ellington, Missouri. Trees began to snap like toothpicks. Within three and a half hours, this twister would become the deadliest in U.S. history. People called it the Tri-State Tornado because it traveled 219 miles (352 km) through three states— Missouri, Illinois, and Indiana.

"Boards, poles, cans, garments, stoves, whole sides of the little frame houses, in some cases the houses themselves, were picked up and smashed to earth," a newspaper reporter wrote about the storm. *"And living beings, too. A baby was blown from its mother's arms. A cow, picked up by the wind, was hurled into the village restaurant."*

Lela Hartman was only four years

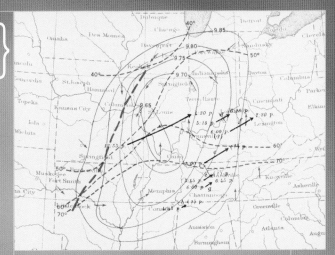

The black line on this chart shows the 1925 Tri-State Tornado's 219-mile (352-km) path.

old when the tornado struck. Lela was visiting her grandmother's farm near West Frankfort, Illinois. *"It just kept getting darker and darker,"* she remembered many years later. *"It was almost as black as night when we finally went to the cellar."* The family was safe in their underground storm cellar. But when they came out, Lela noticed that the storm had done something odd to her grandma's house.

"It . . . turned the house on the foundation," Lela remembered. *"That was a big, big ol' house, and it turned it on the foundation."* The twister lifted the entire house and swung it around so that the front door faced in a different direction.

The air was filled with 10,000 things.

—a reporter for the Saint Louis Post-Dispatch newspaper

Everyone agreed that the Tri-State Tornado was huge. *"It was so wide,"* said Eugene Porter, who lived in Murphysboro, Illinois. F. M. Hewitt, in De Soto, Illinois, described a *"seething, boiling mass of clouds. . . . [and] a roaring noise as of many trains."*

One young girl in Gorham, Illinois, remembered the twister hitting the town's school. *"I can't describe it,"* she said. *"I can't bear to think about it. Children all around me were cut and bleeding. They cried and screamed. It was something awful. I had to close my eyes."*

In all, the Tri-State Tornado killed almost 700 people and injured about 2,000 others. And many thousands lost their homes. The twister destroyed or severely damaged ten towns, including homes, schools, and other buildings.

A public school in De Soto, Illinois, lay in ruins after the massive 1925 tornado swept through.

Tornado Alley

TORNADOES CAN OCCUR IN MANY PLACES AROUND THE WORLD. THE UNITED STATES HAS FAR MORE TORNADOES THAN ANY OTHER COUNTRY. IN FACT, ABOUT THREE-FOURTHS OF ALL TORNADOES IN THE WORLD HIT THE UNITED STATES. TWISTERS CAN HAPPEN IN EVERY STATE. HOWEVER, THEY ARE MOST COMMON IN THE MIDWEST, SOUTHEAST, AND SOUTHWEST.

Tornadoes rarely hit large cities, but that does not make them safe from a storm. This tornado formed over downtown Dallas, Texas, in April 1960.

One area gets so many tornadoes that people call it Tornado Alley. It stretches from North Dakota south to Texas and Louisiana and as far east as Ohio. The weather in Tornado Alley is often perfect for the formation of tornadoes. Warm, moist air masses flow into the area from the Gulf of Mexico. They meet colder, drier air that often flows in from the west and north. When these air masses collide, thunderstorms and tornadoes can result.

Tornadoes have tremendous power. They have been known to drive many objects through trees, such as the record at left.

ANYTIME STORMS

Tornadoes can strike at any time of the year. But most twisters happen during tornado season, which lasts from March through August. The most dangerous months of all are March, April, and May. During that time, the Tornado Alley area is still cool and dry from winter. When wet, warm air flows in from the Gulf of Mexico, storms start to form.

By summertime, the air in most of Tornado Alley has gotten warm. It is closer in temperature to the Gulf of Mexico's air masses. As a result, the number of tornadoes decreases. Tornadoes, however, can form during hurricanes, which continue to occur until late autumn. In September 2004, Hurricane Ivan produced almost one hundred tornadoes.

Tornadoes can also happen at any time of the day. Just like thunderstorms, however, tornadoes are most common in the afternoon and evening. By then the sun has heated up the air. The warm air rises in the updrafts that help form thunderclouds—and sometimes tornadoes.

DID YOU KNOW?

Waterspouts *(above)* are tornadoes that happen over water. They can damage boats, docks, and other structures. Some are tornadoes that formed from storms over land and travel over a lake or other body of water. Others form over the water in fair weather and cause less damage.

DISASTER ZONES

About 75 percent of the world's tornadoes strike in North America's Tornado Alley (shown in red). This map shows where some notable twisters have touched down.

ASIA

Hamburg, Germany
Widecombe-in-the-Moor, England

EUROPE

Dakha, Bangladesh
1969 (540 deaths)

Jessore, Bangladesh
near Ludhiana, India

Central Bangladesh
1996 (more than 600 deaths)

AFRICA

Calcutta, India

New Delhi, India
1978 (28 deaths)

AUSTRALIA

New Richmond, Wisconsin
1889 (119 deaths)

NORTH AMERICA

Flint, Michigan

Xenia, Ohio
Worcester, Massachusetts

Omaha, Nebraska
1975 (more than 4000 buildings damaged)

Limon, Colorado

Tri-State Tornado
1925 (nearly 700 deaths)

St. Louis, Missouri

Western Tenessee

Gainesville, Georgia

Oklahoma Tornado Outbreak
1999 (41 deaths)

Natchez, Mississippi

Pampa, Texas

Marshfield, Missouri

Wichita Falls, Texas
1979 (more than 40 deaths)

SOUTH AMERICA

A worker surveys the tornado damage to a couple's home in Xenia, Ohio.

1974
TORNADO SUPER OUTBREAK

Eight-year-old Rick Hoag was watching television at home in Xenia, Ohio, on April 3, 1974. His mom called from work to tell Rick and his dad that a bad storm was on the way. *"She told me to make sure the garage door was shut and stay inside,"* Rick recalled.

Soon the electricity went out. Rick looked out the window. A whirling column of wind was heading right toward the house. It twisted and turned like a giant snake. One end was high in the sky. The other end touched the ground, tearing apart everything in its path.

"I think back often to that day," Rick said.

As the wind howled, Rick and his dad took shelter in a small bathroom. His dad sat on the floor with his back against the door, bracing his feet against the opposite wall. Then the storm hit, with a roar like a hundred railroad trains. It began tearing the house apart. Windows broke, walls cracked, and wind rushed up under the bathroom floor.

"*I asked [Dad] if we were flying,*" Rick remembered. "*When things calmed down we opened the door.*" Rick and his father saw that much of their house was simply gone. "*The odd feeling I had,*" Rick said, "*looking up the street from inside what once was my hallway, is still with me today.*"

The series of April tornadoes was the worst tornado outbreak in U.S. history. Known as the Super Outbreak, it included 148 tornadoes. They touched down in a 2,500-mile (4,023 km) path of destruction covering thirteen states and parts of Canada. At one point, 15 twisters were on the ground at the same time.

The massive 1974 tornado approaches Xenia, Ohio.

"*The sound was tremendous.*"

—Rick Hoag

Strong winds in the storms picked up cars and mobile homes and carried them away. Wind pulled trees out of the ground. The storms tore apart houses, stores, schools, and other buildings.

All the broken pieces—sharp glass, splinters of wood, bricks, and tree branches—whipped through the air at more than 100 miles per hour (161 km/hr). The debris caused more damage when it hit people and buildings. In sixteen hours, the storms killed 350 people and injured more than 6,000. About 27,500 buildings were damaged. The damage cost more than $600 million.

This house in Xenia was cut in half by the tornado that ripped through the town.

29

Measuring a Menace

WHEN PEOPLE HEAR ABOUT A TORNADO, THEY WONDER WHETHER IT WAS STRONG ENOUGH TO CAUSE A DISASTER. THEY ALSO WANT TO KNOW HOW ITS STRENGTH COMPARED TO TORNADOES IN THE PAST.

After a 1974 tornado in Brandenburg, Kentucky, parents asked those questions as they drove toward the high school to find their children. "All of us were yelling to each other in other cars, asking what had been hit, who had been hurt, where was the worst damage," said Libby Brown. Her daughter was in the school. "And nobody knew."

In the past, people could only guess at how strong a tornado had been. Have you ever heard the expression, "Appearances can be deceiving?" That's true for tornadoes. Big tornadoes can have weak winds and cause little damage. Small tornadoes can be very strong and cause great disasters.

DR. TORNADO

In 1951 T. Theodore Fujita invented a way to measure tornadoes. He was a famous weather scientist who knew so much about twisters that people called him Dr. Tornado. The measuring system is usually called the Fujita scale. Sometimes it is also called the Fujita-Pearson tornado scale after Allen Pearson, another scientist who helped develop it.

Fujita realized that it would be difficult to make direct measurements of tornado winds. Tornadoes last only a short time. They occur without giving much advance warning.

BIGGEST TORNADO

The 1925 Tri-State Tornado in Missouri, Illinois, and Indiana probably was the biggest tornado ever recorded. People said it was more than 1 mile (1.6 km) across. Modern scientists, however, are not sure whether it was one monster twister or a "family" of many tornadoes that came from one storm.

This rubble marks all that is left of a house after a tornado touched down in Worcester, Massachusetts, in June 1953.

And in 1951, it was impossible to send measuring instruments to the places where tornadoes were happening.

Fujita decided to measure the strength of tornadoes by the amount of damage they caused. Fujita knew that only winds of certain strengths could tear roofs off houses, blow down brick walls, and overturn trains. So if a tornado caused such damage, its winds must have been of a certain strength.

INCREDIBLE, INCONCEIVABLE TORNADOES

Theodore Fujita works with a tornado simulator in 1979 in his lab at the University of Chicago.

The Fujita scale goes from F0 to F6. An F0 is the weakest tornado, with winds of 40 to 72 miles per hour (64 to 116 km/hr). This type of twister is strong enough to damage chimneys, break branches off trees, and push over trees with very shallow roots. An F3 tornado has winds of 158 to 206 miles per hour (254 to 332 km/hr). These winds can overturn railroad trains, tear roofs off houses, and topple trees with deep roots.

An F5 on the Fujita scale is an "incredible tornado." With winds of 261 to 318 miles per hour (420 to 512 km/hr), it can throw automobiles more than 325 feet (99 m)—farther than the length of a football field.

Dr. Tornado saved F6 for the "inconceivable tornado." With winds up to 379 miles per hour (610 km/hr), it would destroy almost everything in its path. Such a tornado has never been recorded, but it is possible.

The Fujita scale depends on the judgment of people who check the damage. It takes highly trained individuals to make a judgment. Different people may make

FASTEST WINDS

The fastest winds ever measured in a tornado were 318 miles per hour (512 km/hr). A car going that fast could travel 5 miles (8 km) in just one minute. Joshua Wurman, a tornado researcher at the University of Oklahoma, measured the wind speed during a May 3, 1999, twister near Oklahoma City.

THE ENHANCED FUJITA SCALE

IN FEBRUARY 2007, SCIENTISTS WILL BEGIN USING AN UPDATED FUJITA SCALE WITH REFINED WIND SPEEDS. TORNADOES THAT HAPPENED IN THE PAST WILL NOT BE RE-CATEGORIZED, BUT ALL FUTURE TORNADOES WILL BE RANKED ACCORDING TO THIS ENHANCED FUJITA SCALE.

CATEGORY	WIND SPEED	TYPE OF DAMAGE
EF0	65–85 MPH (105–137 KM/HR)	LIGHT DAMAGE. SOME DAMAGE TO CHIMNEYS; BRANCHES BROKEN OFF TREES; SHALLOW-ROOTED TREES PUSHED OVER.
EF1	86–110 MPH (138–177 KM/HR)	MOBILE HOMES OVERTURNED; MOVING CARS PUSHED OFF ROADS; ATTACHED GARAGES MAY BE DESTROYED.
EF2	111–135 MPH (179–217 KM/HR)	ROOFS TORN OFF SOME HOUSES; MOBILE HOMES DEMOLISHED; TRAIN BOXCARS OVERTURNED; LARGE TREES UPROOTED.
EF3	136–165 MPH (219–266 KM/HR)	ROOFS AND SOME WALLS TORN OFF STRONG HOUSES; TRAINS OVERTURNED; MOST TREES UPROOTED; HEAVY CARS LIFTED OFF GROUND AND THROWN.
EF4	166–200 MPH (237–322 KM/HR)	STRONG HOUSES LEVELED; WEAKER HOUSES BLOWN AWAY SOME DISTANCE; CARS THROWN.
EF5	MORE THAN 200 MPH (MORE THAN 322 KM/HR)	STRONG HOUSES LIFTED OFF FOUNDATIONS AND CARRIED CONSIDERABLE DISTANCES; CARS THROWN MORE THAN 325 FEET (99 M); BARK TORN OFF TREES; INCREDIBLE THINGS WILL OCCUR.

A tornado forms near Red Rock, Oklahoma, in May 2003. }

different judgments. To make the Fujita scale more accurate, February 2007 a revised scale will be used.

Fortunately, about 74 percent of all tornadoes are the relatively weak F0 or F1 storms. About 25 percent are F2 or F3. Only 1 percent are the very violent F4 and F5 storms. But forecasters can't predict the strength of a tornado in advance. That makes it important for people to take each tornado seriously. It may be an F0 or an F5.

TORNADO TURTLES

One of the most important tools for measuring strong storms and tornadoes is Doppler radar. Radar uses invisible radio waves to locate objects. Doppler radar is a special kind of radar. It can show and measure wind directions and wind speeds. Doppler radar images can tell forecasters when a tornado is forming inside a mesocyclone.

Another tool is the anemometer, which measures wind speeds. This instrument has little cups that catch the wind. Then the cups spin around at speeds that show the strength of the wind.

But an anemometer cannot take measurements inside a tornado. The strong winds would tear the instrument apart. So scientists sometimes use tools called turtles. These turtles are packages of instruments covered with armor, like an army tank. Scientists leave them in the storm's path, where they can get sucked right up into a twister without breaking. Turtles measure air pressure, temperature, and moisture levels.

THE NOAA
The NOAA is the National Oceanic and Atmospheric Administration. It is part of the U.S. government, and it includes the National Weather Service. The Weather Service forecasts weather conditions. NOAA also does scientific research on better ways to predict and respond to tornadoes and other severe weather.

U.S. DEPT. OF COMMERCE
WEATHER BUREAU
EXPERIMENTAL TORNADO DETECTION RADAR

This Doppler radar unit was the first one used by the Weather Bureau. The Bureau was an early form of the National Weather Service.

"There was nothing that was recognizable. **Nothing!**"

—Ron Wert, describing the destruction of an F5 tornado that hit western Michigan in 1956

The 1956 tornado turned this Michigan field into a junkyard. Homes smashed to pieces and vehicles turned on their sides were only part of the damage done by the violent storm.

1979 WICHITA FALLS TORNADO

The devastation in Wichita Falls, Texas, following the 1979 F5 tornado was widespread.

On Tuesday, April 10, the tornado sirens of Wichita Falls, Texas, cried out a warning. People expected an ordinary twister. But what they got was a monster that measured up to 1.5 miles (2.4 km) across.

Wilma Rickard and a friend were at a shopping center with their children when the tornado hit. She remembered that the wind *"blew and it blew and it blew. One second it felt like it was going to flatten you like a pancake. . . . And then, the next second, it felt like it was going to pick you up and throw you through the roof. And it would do that over and over and over.*

"Then it stopped. We got up. I realized all the rain I thought was going to drown us was really debris

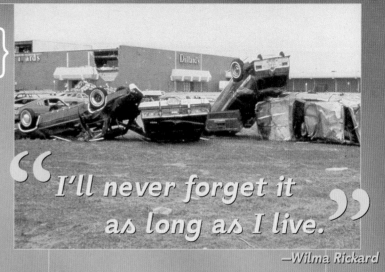

The massive Wichita Falls tornado stacked these cars on top of one another.

" *I'll never forget it as long as I live.* "

—Wilma Rickard

hitting us. . . . I then saw the wall in front of me. Most of it was gone. It had pipes with water spraying out everywhere. And you could smell gas. My friend was bloody, but the kids and I were fine."

Other people were not so lucky. Some tried to escape the tornado in their cars. The wind blew cars off the road and stacked them up one on top of another in the shopping center parking lot.

"The suffering and destruction caused by the Wichita Falls tornado is nearly inconceivable," a National Weather Service meteorologist wrote in his report. *"The passage of a violent tornado through an 8-mile [13 km] section of a city is an almost*

The 1979 twister upended many heavy objects, such as cars, as if they weighed nothing.

unheard-of natural disaster."

The twister was the worst of thirteen tornadoes that snaked through the Red River valley that day, hitting Texas, Oklahoma, and Arkansas. Advance warnings saved many people's lives. But in Wichita Falls alone, the tornado killed more than 40 people and injured about 1,800. The twister also destroyed or damaged more than 5,000 homes, causing $400 million in damage. People still call that day Terrible Tuesday.

People Helping People

IN A DISASTER, PEOPLE FIRST FEEL SHOCK AND NUMBNESS. THEY MIGHT NOT EVEN BELIEVE THAT A TWISTER IS ROARING TOWARD THEIR HOME OR SCHOOL. PEOPLE FEAR FOR THEIR OWN SAFETY AND FOR THAT OF FAMILY, FRIENDS, AND PETS. THEY WANT TO FIND A SAFE PLACE TO TAKE SHELTER.

People who survive a disaster often need help to recover. Recovery means getting life back to normal again. Tornadoes and other disasters may kill or injure family members, friends, and pets. Survivors feel grief for the injured and dead. Disasters also can destroy peoples' homes and everything that they owned.

"What we saw has never left me since," remembered Lisa Irene Hale. She was just ten years old during the great 1974 tornado outbreak. Lisa and her mother took shelter in a grocery store in Xenia, Ohio. After the tornado passed, Lisa remembered, "there were people walking in the street, but no one said a word. It was a deafening, numbing silence."

Survivors of a tornado disaster need water, food, clothing, and warm blankets. They may also need a place to live until new homes can be built. Wreckage must be cleared away so new buildings can be constructed. Workers must restore electricity and telephone service.

Shop owners in Pierce City, Missouri, embrace after their businesses were damaged by a 2003 tornado.

38

A woman in Moore, Oklahoma, took a break from tornado cleanup in May 2003.

NEIGHBORS HELPING NEIGHBORS

Tornadoes usually affect only a small area. That makes it easier for help to arrive from outside the disaster area. But at first, people may have to help themselves and one another. That can be difficult right after disaster strikes. People affected by a twister are often in a state of shock.

"People were walking, dazed and hushed," said Jim Brocker, who was in La Plata, Maryland, minutes after a 2002 tornado. "In the stillness, one woman ran screaming toward a damaged motel. People tried to stop her, ask her if she was OK, but she just kept running and screaming."

Still, neighbors have always helped neighbors. "My father left immediately to help in gathering up and caring for the wounded," said W. D. Chitty, remembering the 1880 tornado in Marshfield, Missouri. The tornado destroyed the Chittys' house. But his family worked hard to help others after the twister.

DISASTER RELIEF WORKERS

Help from outside is also very important after a tornado strikes. Assistance may come from disaster relief teams sent by the Federal Emergency Management Agency (FEMA), part of the U.S. government. Help also might arrive from fire departments in other cities or from the U.S. military's National Guard. Private organizations such as the Salvation Army also send help. Within hours of a disaster, their airplanes can fly in huge loads of supplies and hundreds of experienced workers.

When a disaster strikes a poor region, people there may not have enough resources to recover. That's when help from the outside is especially important.

STORM SPOTTERS

The National Weather Service needs help to spot twisters ahead of time. Many areas of Tornado Alley have networks of specially trained people who swing into action during a tornado watch. This group of storm spotters is called the SKYWARN Network.

Storm spotters who see a tornado alert the Weather Service so that it can issue a tornado warning. Their sharp eyes and training have saved many lives.

FEMA agents surveyed tornado damage in Lexington, Kentucky, after a twister tore through the town in 2004.

Other countries and private relief organizations may send disaster relief teams and supplies. The International Red Cross and Red Crescent Movement is also a major source of aid.

Ordinary people also donate money or volunteer to help tornado victims. In 1880 W. D. Chitty remembered that "the whole world seemed to respond in sympathy and practical generosity to stricken little Marshfield. Within forty-eight hours the sidings [railroad tracks] were crowded with trains bearing nurses, doctors, medicines, food, clothing, and everything essential for the immediate relief of the victims."

HOW CAN YOU HELP?

One of the best ways to help people affected by a disaster is to donate money to an organization that is helping the victims. Money allows those organizations to buy exactly what they need. The American Red Cross (www.redcross.org) often is among the first organizations to arrive at a disaster scene in the United States.

At first, relief workers may start by providing emergency medical help to injured people. They may also help rescue workers find people trapped in the wreckage of buildings. Later, they often help people set up shelters in schools and other big buildings. Tornado disaster victims whose homes have been damaged or destroyed can stay at these shelters for a few days.

GETTING A LIFE BACK

Victims of tornadoes and other disasters often need money to get their lives back to normal. That is especially important when a tornado destroys much of a town, as the 1974 twister in Xenia, Ohio, did. When businesses, factories, and farms are destroyed, many people are left with no place to work. That makes it hard for them to earn money until the damage is repaired.

"Where we ever got the money to rebuild so promptly has always been a mystery," Chitty said about Marshfield. "But the fact is that little time was lost in restoring the town to its former business capacity."

The people of Xenia also rebuilt their town. They got help from the U.S. government, through special loans to disaster victims. Starting over is not easy. But most communities damaged by tornadoes do rebuild eventually. People do get a life back again.

Canine (dog) search crews gather outside a collapsed
building in Pierce City, Missouri, where citizens had
been seeking shelter from violent storms. The dogs
helped search for survivors of a series of tornadoes
that had swept through the town in 2003.

A woman weeps after a tornado leveled her home in Bangladesh in 1996.

1996
DISASTER IN BANGLADESH

In 1996 Babul Ahmed was ten years old. He and his family lived in Rampur, a village in Bangladesh. This southern Asian country is near India. On the evening of May 13, Babul's family knew a storm was brewing when the wind started blowing and rain poured down. But they didn't expect a tornado.

With winds whirling up to 125 miles per hour (201 km/hr), the tornado tore buildings apart as if they were built from sand. *"It was dust and wind everywhere,"* said Babul. The winds picked up people, farm animals, and carts as if they were feathers. About 55 of Babul's neighbors died. Hundreds more were injured. *"We heard cries for help from everywhere but could see nothing,"* said one man.

Relatives surround the bodies of loved ones, victims of the 1996 twister that killed nearly 500 people and injured more than 30,000 others.

The whole village has diminished into a vast grave.

—a police officer in the village of Barabhita, not far from Rampur

As the twister came roaring toward another village, people ran into the police station. Bangladesh is a poor country, where many families live crowded together in small houses. Those homes are often poorly built out of rickety materials. They would fall apart easily in the tornado's winds. The police station was the strongest building in the village. People thought they would be safe there. But the tornado's winds were too strong even for that building. In all, more than 100 people died in that village.

The tornado continued to rip through central Bangladesh, striking 80 villages other than Babul's. In the whole disaster zone, more than 600 people were killed and tens of thousands were injured. Local hospitals were soon overflowing with patients. They ran out of medicine, bandages, and other supplies. Some injured people waited hours or days for a doctor or nurse. Others died because there were not enough emergency workers to help.

The tornado completely destroyed at least 10,000 houses, damaging thousands of others. More than 100,000 people were left homeless. The storm also snapped telephone lines and uprooted trees. It destroyed farmers' crops and killed cows and other farm animals. And even after the tornado passed, it took days for help to arrive. When it did, residents of the ruined towns began to rebuild their lives. But they would never be the same.

The Future

"ATTENTION! A TORNADO WILL FORM NEAR SMITHBURG BETWEEN NINE AND ELEVEN O'CLOCK TONIGHT. BY MIDNIGHT IT WILL MOVE DOWN MAIN STREET. THEN IT WILL GO DOWN HIGHWAY 86 TOWARD THE NEW TOWN SHOPPING CENTER. EVERYONE IN THOSE AREAS SHOULD LEAVE OR TAKE COVER."

Weather forecasters wish they could give people that kind of advance warning about tornadoes. They could save many lives if they could tell, hours ahead of time, whether a tornado will form, when it will hit, and where it will go. The more advance warning people have, the better they can prepare for a disaster. But this kind of detailed information is still in the future.

In the past, people had little or no warning. Sometimes they just looked out the window and saw a tornado approaching. Other times, they heard a roar like a train and suddenly found that a tornado was right in their backyard. Even with modern technology, warnings do not always come in time. "I heard something and I thought it was hail," said Chuck Smith, who was at work in Stoneville, North Carolina, in 1998 when a twister hit without warning. "Then, two seconds later, the roof started lifting off."

By studying past storms, scientists and weather forecasters have learned a lot about what might happen in future tornadoes. They know, for example, the weather conditions that can produce tornadoes. When they notice such conditions, the National Weather Service Storm Prediction Center in Norman, Oklahoma, alerts the public so people can prepare.

A Doppler radar station in Norman, Oklahoma

"Your mind could not accept what you were seeing. It couldn't be— but it was."

—Lisa Irene Hale, recalling the 1974 Super Outbreak

{ A tornado approached this Oklahoma City house in July 1980.

WATCHES AND WARNINGS

People learn about severe weather alerts from television, regular radio, special weather radios, and the Internet. There are two kinds of tornado alerts—watches and warnings. A tornado watch means that weather conditions are right for a tornado. It tells people to stay tuned for further information. Watches usually last two to six hours and cover an area of up to thousands of square miles.

A tornado warning means that a tornado has actually been spotted. It tells people to take cover immediately. Some cities turn on a special warning siren to make sure everyone knows about the danger. Most tornado warnings cover small areas, such as a county or city, and usually last less than an hour.

This military airplane was damaged in a 1948 tornado that swept through Tinker Air Force Base in Oklahoma. The first broadcast tornado warning occurred during this storm.

BETTER TORNADO TECHNOLOGY

After the devastating 1974 Tornado Super Outbreak, the National Weather Service realized that it needed better technology to detect tornadoes. The Weather Service spent about $4.5 billion to modernize weather forecasting technology.

"What we saw [in 1974] as a green blob on [an old] radar scope is now depicted in full color and high resolution detail," said John Forsing. He helped forecast the Super Outbreak for the Weather Service. "With modernized technology such as Doppler radar, weather satellites, and advanced computers, forecasters can now pinpoint tornadoes even before they touch down."

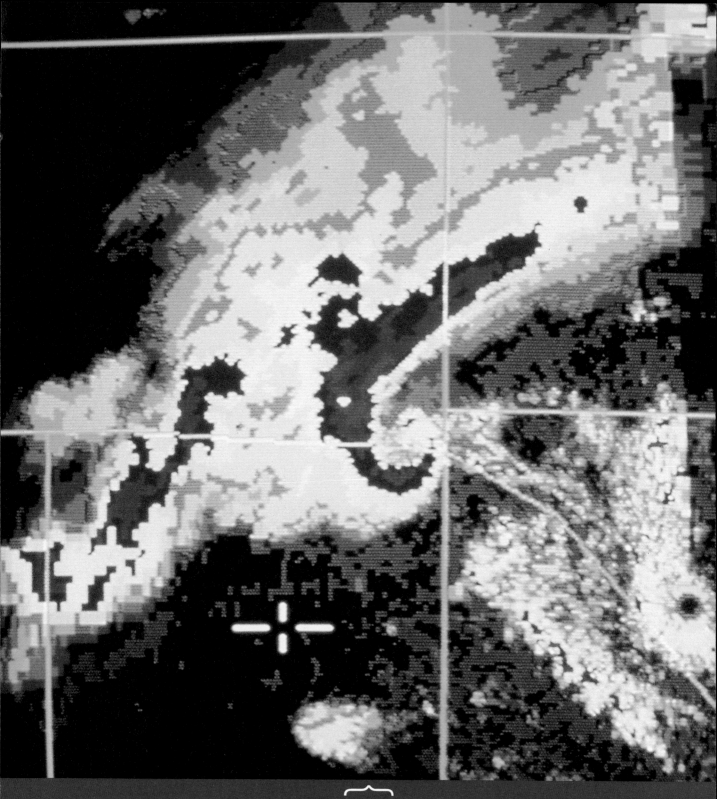

This radar screen shows a hook echo, a type of storm
formation that often leads to tornadoes.

With help from these new tools, the National Weather Service issues about fifteen thousand severe storm and tornado watches and warnings each year. New technology and better scientific knowledge allow forecasters to issue those warnings sooner. People usually have about twelve minutes advance notice of severe weather. That is twice as much time as they had as recently as the mid-1990s.

People also get more accurate alerts than they used to. In 1974 forecasts were only half as accurate as they are in the early twenty-first century.

Computers help weather forecasters tell when severe storms will happen. In the future, more powerful computers will probably produce even better forecasts. They will give individuals and communities more time to prepare for tornadoes. This extra time is very important. It helps save lives and can also reduce the amount of property damage.

BE PREPARED

Have you ever heard the expression, "Forewarned is forearmed?" It means that if you know what's about to happen, you can prepare yourself for it.

A home disaster plan is important in preparing for tornadoes. Families should pick a place at home where everyone can go if a tornado approaches. Some families in

These students are practicing tornado safety—crouching against a solid, interior wall and protecting their heads. Most schools perform such drills to prepare students in the event of a real disaster.

Ten neighbors in Moore, Oklahoma, were trapped for more than an hour in this storm shelter. A 2003 tornado had swept through the town, blocking the shelter's exit with debris.

Tornado Alley have underground tornado shelters or safe rooms. These specially built spaces can withstand up to 250-mile-per-hour winds (402 km/hr) and 100-mile-per-hour hits (161 km/hr) by flying debris. They survive even if the rest of the house is flattened.

The basement also can be a safe place. If a house has no basement, use a bathroom, center hallway, or closet on the lowest story. Stay away from windows and try to hide under a mattress or sturdy piece of furniture.

Whole communities should also prepare for tornadoes. Many tornadoes strike when people are asleep and not listening to television or radio warnings. A community tornado siren can wake up sleeping people and save lives. Sirens and shelters can be especially important in mobile home communities, where tornadoes often cause great damage. Mobile homes should be anchored securely to the ground. And people living in mobile home parks should know about separate shelters in their communities. These shelters are built specifically to keep people safe during tornadoes and other emergencies.

TORNADO MYTHS & FACTS

MYTH: Open windows in your house, or it will explode as the vacuum inside a tornado sucks up air outside.
FACT: Don't waste the time. Instead, head for shelter. The wind and debris from a tornado will probably break the windows.

MYTH: The southwest corner of your basement is the safest place during a tornado.
FACT: Tornadoes often come from the southwest, so that may be the most dangerous place to hide. The very safest place is a basement room with no windows and sturdy walls.

MYTH: Tornadoes never strike big cities.
FACT: Tornadoes are relatively rare in big cities, but no place has natural protection from a tornado. Twisters have hit large cities such as Oklahoma City, Oklahoma; Miami, Florida; Fort Worth, Texas; Nashville, Tennessee; and Salt Lake City, Utah.

A September 2005 tornado in Minnesota tore part of the roof off this couple's home. In the Upper Midwest, it is extremely rare to experience tornadoes so late in the season.

New construction methods are being used to build stronger homes and other buildings. For example, special tornado clips keep roofs attached to buildings when a tornado tries to suck them up. Better ways of attaching mobile homes to the ground are important too.

Tornadoes are frightening, and they can cause terrible disasters. Being prepared, however, is much better than being scared. The more information people have about tornadoes, the better they will understand the threat— and the better able they will be to protect themselves if a twister ever hits.

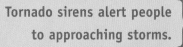
Tornado sirens alert people to approaching storms.

TORNADO SAFETY RULES

You and your family can stay safe during a tornado emergency by following a few simple rules.

DURING A TORNADO WATCH:

- Listen to local radio and television stations for updates.

- Watch the weather nearby. Strong winds or a roaring sound like a freight train may mean a tornado is approaching.

DURING A TORNADO WARNING:

- If you are inside, go to the safe place that you and your family picked in advance to protect yourself from glass and other flying objects.

- If you are outside, lie flat in a ditch or low-lying area, or hurry to the basement of the closest sturdy building.

- If you are in a car or mobile home, get out. Head for one of the safe places above.

AFTER A TORNADO PASSES:

- Watch for fallen electric power lines. Do not touch any that you find.

- Stay out of the damaged area.

- Listen to the radio for information and instructions.

- Do not light matches or candles. They could cause explosions or fires if natural gas is leaking into the air.

Timeline

1638 A tornado hits Widecombe-in-the-Moor, England.

1643 Wind described as a "sudden gust" strikes Massachusetts. This wind may have been the first tornado recorded in North America.

1840 The Great Natchez Tornado strikes Mississippi, killing at least 317 people.

1880 A tornado, spotted by W. D. Chitty, destroys much of Marshfield, Missouri.

1882 A tornado in Iowa kills more than 100 people.

1884 About 800 people are killed by a series of 60 tornadoes sweeping through the southeastern United States *(right)*.

1889 A single tornado is responsible for the deaths of 119 citizens in New Richmond, Wisconsin.

1896 Approximately 300 citizens of Saint Louis, Missouri, are killed by a powerful twister.

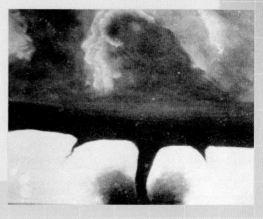

1925 The Tri-State Tornado, the deadliest tornado in U.S. history, strikes Missouri, Illinois, and Indiana, killing nearly 700 people.

1936 Several twisters race through the southern United States in early April. One strikes Gainesville, Georgia *(left)*, killing more than 100 people. Gainesville was also hit directly in 1903 and would be hit again in 1944.

1948 The first tornado forecast is made. Forecasting leads to tornado observation and prediction centers, saving thousands of lives each year.

1951 Theodore Fujita invents a scale to measure the intensity of tornadoes.

1953 A June 8 tornado near Flint, Michigan *(facing page, top)*, kills more than 100 people and demolishes hundreds of homes. The storm moves eastward and forms another tornado in Massachusetts on June 9. This twister kills dozens, covers 46

miles (74 km), and spends 90 minutes on the ground. Debris is swept eastward into Massachusetts Bay and the Atlantic Ocean.

1965 More than 36 tornadoes strike the midwestern United States, killing more than 250 people.

1969 A twister in Dakha, Bangladesh (then East Pakistan), kills 540 people and leaves 80,000 homeless.

1974 The Super Tornado Outbreak sweeps across the Midwest.

1975 Early tornado warnings provided by volunteer radio operators save many lives when a twister hits Omaha, Nebraska.

1979 The Wichita Falls, Texas, tornado causes $400 million in damage. An early warning system saves most citizens.

1985 On May 31, a series of 41 tornadoes strikes the northeastern United States, causing 90 deaths.

1990 A tornado destroys most of Limon, Colorado, causing $12 million in damages.

1991 An outbreak of more than 50 tornadoes strikes six states in the Midwest.

1995 A small but powerful tornado in Pampa, Texas, causes $30 million in damage *(right)*.

1996 A tornado in Bangladesh kills at least 600 people.

1999 In one day, 59 tornadoes touch down in central Oklahoma.

2003 During a single week in early May, approximately 400 tornadoes strike in the United States.

2004 September's Hurricane Ivan sparks dozens of tornadoes.

2005 A tornado strikes Kentucky and southern Indiana *(left)* at about 2 A.M. on November 6, killing 24 people and injuring more than 200.

2006 More than 50 tornadoes sweep through 8 states in the Midwest and South, killing at least 27 people.

Glossary

debris: pieces of buildings or other things that have been destroyed. Tornadoes pick up debris such as bricks, wooden beams, and broken glass.

Doppler radar: a special kind of radar that shows and measures wind directions and speeds. Doppler readings help scientists and weather forecasters learn about the formation and movement of tornadoes.

mesocyclone: spinning air inside a supercell. Some mesocyclones produce tornadoes.

meteorologist: a scientist who studies the weather

supercell: a severe thunderstorm with strong winds

tornado warning: a weather alert when a tornado has been spotted in the area or has shown up on local radar. During a warning, people should take cover.

tornado watch: a weather alert given when conditions in a region are right for producing tornadoes. During a watch, a tornado has not yet been spotted.

updraft: a rising current of air

wall cloud: a spinning cloud formation that hangs down from a supercell and looks like a dark wall of clouds hanging in the sky. Some wall clouds produce tornadoes.

waterspout: a funnel cloud that forms over a body of water

weather front: the boundary where two masses of air with different conditions meet

wind shear: a change or difference in wind speed, direction, or both. In a supercell, wind shear can create a wide, horizontal tube of rapidly spinning air.

Places to Visit

These science centers present exhibits and other information about tornadoes. Visit to find out more!

Carnegie Science Center—Pittsburgh, Pennsylvania
http://www.carnegiesciencecenter.org
At this museum, you can create your own 4-foot-tall (1.2 m) tornado by regulating the flow of cool and warm air in a special chamber.

The Pacific Museum of the Earth—Vancouver, British Columbia, Canada
http://www.eos.ubc.ca/public/museum/visitorinfo.html#address
This museum has a permanent exhibit on tornadoes.

Weather Museum—Houston, Texas
http://www.wxresearch.com/museum
Visit the Weather Research Center at this museum to find out how to walk safely through a tornado!

Source Notes

4   Cable News Network, "Tornado Kills 22 in Indiana," *CNN.com*, November 7, 2005, http://www.cnn.com/2005/WEATHER/11/06/indiana.tornadoes/ (January 10, 2006).

4   WorldNow and WFIE, "Historic Tornado Outbreak Sunday," *WFIE*, November 6, 2005, http://www.14wfie.com/Global/story.asp?S=4077888 (January 10, 2006).

4   Ibid.

4   CNN, "Tornado Kills 22 in Indiana."

4   Reuters, "23 Dead in US Tornado Destruction," *ABC News Online*, November 8, 2005, http://www.abc.net.au/news/newsitems/200511/s1499955.htm (January 31, 2006).

5   Cable News Network, "'The Whole House Just Exploded,'" *CNN.com*, November 8, 2005, http://www.cnn.com/2005/WEATHER/11/07/tornado/ (January 10, 2006).

6   Mark Scolforo, "Tornado Survivors Recount Harrowing Tales," *phillyBurbs.com*, July 15, 2004, http://www.phillyburbs.com/pb-dyn/news/103-07152004-331825.html (October 17, 2005).

8   Homer G. Ramby, "Don E. Halsey–Meteorologists," *Xenia Tornado*, n.d., http://www.xeniatornado.com/vwso.htm (October 17, 2005).

9   Scott Koerner, "Survivor Stories from Brandenburg," *Tornado Super Outbreak–April 3, 1974*, n.d., http://www.april31974.com/survivor_stories_from_brandenburg.htm (October 17, 2005).

10   UAW Local 2209, "Oklahoma City GM Plant Tornado Damage," *UAW Local 2209*, May 9, 2003, http://www.local2209.org/default100b.asp (October 17, 2005).

10   "Marshfield Missouri–Tornado," *Sho-Me Power Electric Cooperative*, n.d., http://www.shomepower.com/tornado.htm (October 17, 2005).

12–13 Ibid.

13   Ibid.

14   NOAA, "Cold Front Spawns Super-Cell Storms, Deadly Tornadoes in Central Plains States," *NOAA News Online*, May 5, 2003, http://www.noaanews.noaa.gov/stories/s1136.htm (October 17, 2005).

22   NOAA, "Interesting Quotes," 1925 *Tri-State Tornado: A Look Back*, 2005, http://www.crh.noaa.gov/pah/1925/iq_body.html (October 17, 2005).

22–23 Ibid.

23   Ibid.

23   Lee Davis, *Natural Disasters*, New York: Facts on File, 2002, 314.

23   NOAA, "Interesting Quotes."

23   Ibid.

28   Homer G. Ramby, "Rick Hoag," *Xenia Tornado*, n.d., http://www.xeniatornado.com/hoag.htm (October 17, 2005).

29   Ibid.

30   Scott Koerner, "Survivor Stories from Brandenburg."

31   WorldNow and WOODTV, "1956: Michigan's Most Destructive Tornado," *WOODTV.com*, n.d., http://www.woodtv.com/Global/story.asp?S=759210 (January 10, 2006).

36   Justin L. and Niki M., "Survivors' Stories," *Twisters: Destruction from the Sky*, n.d., http://library.thinkquest.org/4232/survivor.htm (October 17, 2005).

37   NOAA, "Interesting Quotes."

37   Justin L. and Niki M., "Survivors' Stories."

38   Homer G. Ramby, "Lisa Irene (Pagett) Hale," *Xenia Tornado*, n.d., http://www.xeniatornado.com/hale.htm (October 17, 2005).

40   Jim Brocker and Conni James, "An Eyewitness Account of the Tornado's Devastation," *Gazette.net*, May 1, 2002, http://gazette.net/gazette_archive/2002/200218/montgomerycty/state/102300-1.html (October 17, 2005).

40   "Marshfield Missouri," *Sho-Me Power*.

42   Ibid.

42   Ibid.

44   Cable News Network, "Aid Rushed to Bangladesh Tornado Victims," *CNN.com*, May 15, 1996, http://www.cnn.com/WORLD/9605/15/bangladesh (October 17, 2005).

44   Cable News Network, "Tornado Kills More Than 400 in Bangladesh," *CNN.com*, May 14, 1996, http://www.cnn.com/WORLD/9605/14/bangladesh/index.html (October 17, 2005).

45   Ibid.

46   Taft Wireback, "Survivors Tell Their Tornado Tales," *News & Record Online*, March 21, 1998, http://www.news-record.com/news/indepth/tornado/survivor.shtml (January 10, 2006).

47   Homer G. Ramby, "Lisa Irene (Pagett) Hale."

48   National Oceanic and Atmospheric Administration, "Weather Service Commemorates Nation's Worst Tornado Outbreak," *NOAA and the 1974 Tornado Outbreak*, n.d., http://www.publicaffairs.noaa.gov/storms/release.html (October 17, 2005).

Selected Bibliography

Akin, Wallace E. *The Forgotten Storm: The Great Tri-State Tornado of 1925*. Guilford, CT: Lyons Press, 2002.

Allaby, Michael. *A Chronology of Weather: Dangerous Weather*. New York: Facts on File, Inc., 1998.

Bedard, Richard. *In The Shadow of the Tornado: Stories and Adventures from the Heart of Storm Country*. Norman, OK: Gilco Publishing, 1996.

Bradford, Marlene. *Scanning the Skies: A History of Tornado Forecasting*. Norman: University of Oklahoma Press, 2001.

Capella, Chris. "Tornadoes Are Earth's Most Violent Storms." *USATODAY.com*. May 17, 2005. http://www.usatoday.com/weather/resources/basics/twist0.htm (October 12, 2005).

Centers for Disease Control and Prevention. "Tornadoes." *Emergency Preparedness and Response: Natural Disasters and Severe Weather*. 2003. http://www.bt.cdc.gov/disasters/tornadoes/index.asp (October 12, 2005).

Davidson, Keay. *Twister: The Science of Tornadoes and the Making of an Adventure Movie*. New York: Pocket Books, 1996.

Davis, Lee. *Natural Disasters*. New York: Facts on File, 2002.

Edwards, Roger. "The Online Tornado FAQ." *NOAA's National Weather Service: Storm Prediction Center*. N.d. http://www.spc.noaa.gov/faq/tornado/index.html (October 12, 2005).

Hancock, Paul L., and Brian J. Skinner, eds. *The Oxford Companion to the Earth*. New York: Oxford University Press, 2000.

Hemingway, Lorian. *A World Turned Over: A Killer Tornado and the Lives It Changed Forever*. New York: Simon & Schuster, 2002.

National Oceanic and Atmospheric Administration. "Eyewitness Account: Bobby Boyd." *NOAA and the 1974 Tornado Outbreak*. N.d. http://www.publicaffairs.noaa.gov/storms/boyd.html (October 12, 2005).

——. *Thunderstorms . . . Tornadoes . . . Lightning: Nature's Most Violent Storms.* N.d. http://www.nws.noaa.gov/om/brochures/ttl.pdf (October 12, 2005).

Newson, Lesley. *Devastation! The World's Worst Natural Disasters.* New York: Dorling Kindersley Publishing, 1998.

Pearson Education. "U.S. Tornadoes." *Infoplease.* N.d. http://infoplease.com/ipa/A0001445.html (October 12, 2005).

Robinson, Andrew. *Earth Shock: Hurricanes, Volcanoes, Earthquakes, Tornadoes and Other Forces of Nature.* London: Thames & Hudson, 2002.

Rosenfeld, Jeffrey. *Eye of the Storm: Inside the World's Deadliest Hurricanes, Tornadoes and Blizzards.* New York: Plenum Trade, 1999.

University of Wisconsin Board of Regents. "Tornado Disaster: 39 Dead." *Twister: The Tornado Story.* 2003. http://whyfiles.org/013tornado/2.html (October 12, 2005).

Ward. Kaari, ed. *Great Disasters: Dramatic True Stories of Nature's Awesome Powers.* Pleasantville, NY: Reader's Digest Association, 1989.

Further Resources

BOOKS

Baum, L. Frank. *The Wonderful Wizard of Oz.* Chicago: G. M. Hill Co., 1900.
This book tells the fictional story of Dorothy and her dog, Toto, who are transported to the magical land of Oz by a tornado.

Beard, Darleen Bailey. *Twister.* New York: Farrar, Straus, Giroux, 1999.
In this novel, Lucille and Natt take shelter in the cellar as a tornado approaches and their mother leaves them to help a neighbor.

Berger, Melvin, and Gilda Berger. *Do Tornadoes Really Twist? Questions and Answers about Tornadoes and Hurricanes.* New York: Scholastic Inc., 2000.
This book gives many facts and answers questions about tornadoes and hurricanes.

Challoner, Jack. *Hurricane & Tornado.* New York: Dorling Kindersley, 2000.
Find out about dangerous weather around the world and some facts about famous natural disasters.

Dixon, Franklin W. *The Chase for the Mystery Twister.* New York: Pocket Books, 1998.
The Hardy Boys travel to Oklahoma to study tornadoes.

Erickson, John R. *The Case of the Swirling Killer Tornado.* Houston: Gulf Publishing, 1995.
This is a silly story about Hank and Drover, inside a tornado.

Kramer, Stephen P. *Eye of the Storm: Chasing Storms with Warren Faidley.* New York: G. P. Putnam's Sons, 1997.
This exciting book, with color photographs of wild weather, is accompanied by information about storms.

Lindop, Laurie. *Chasing Tornadoes.* Minneapolis: Twenty-First Century Books, 2003.
Join storm chasers on the hunt in this exciting book!

Maslin, Mark. *Storms.* Austin, TX: Raintree Steck-Vaughn, 2000.
Find out about all different kinds of storms and how they are predicted.

McMullan, Kate. *A Fine Start: Meg's Prairie Diary.* New York: Scholastic, 2003.
This Dear America story is about Meg's life with her family in Kansas and the various weather conditions that they encounter.

Osborne, Mary Pope. *Twister on Tuesday*. New York: Random House, 2001.
   Jack and Annie from the Magic Tree House series go back in time to save their classmates from a tornado.

Osborne, Will, and Mary Pope Osborne. *Twisters and other Terrible Storms*. New York: Random House, 2003.
   This is a research guide to finding out about storms and weather.

Prigger, Mary Skillings. *Aunt Minnie and the Twister*. New York: Clarion Books, 2002.
   Aunt Minnie McGranahan is raising nine orphaned children when a twister strikes and turns their home around!

Simon, Seymour. *Tornadoes*. New York: Morrow Junior Books, 1999.
   Beautiful photos of tornadoes, nature's most violent force, are accompanied by easily understood text.

Vesilind, Priit J. "Chasing Tornadoes." *National Geographic Magazine*, April 2004, 8–37.
   Follow the storm chasers as they search for twisters along Tornado Alley in the American Midwest.

Woods, Michael, and Mary B. Woods. *Hurricanes*. Minneapolis: Lerner Publications Company, 2007.
   Discover hurricanes, disastrous windstorms that are in the cyclone family with tornadoes.

WEBSITES AND FILMS

National Geographic: Eye in the Sky—Tornadoes
   http://www.nationalgeographic.com/eye/tornadoes/tornadoes.html
   The "Eye in the Sky" shows a twister and its aftermath in graphic detail.

1953 Beecher Tornado—The Science Behind the Tornado
   http://www.crh.noaa.gov/dtx/1953beecher/metIntroduction.php
   The year 1953 was one of the worst tornado years in the United States. This site gives plenty of information about the Flint, Michigan, storm of 1953.

Sky Diary KIDSTORM
   http://skydiary.com/kids
   Find facts about violent storms including tornadoes and hurricanes.

SKYWARN National Home Page
   http://www.skywarn.org
   Visit this site, from an organization of storm spotters and chasers, to see many maps of U.S. weather conditions. The SKYWARN Network helps alert local emergency management agencies about possible twisters and other threats.

Tornadoes—Dan's Wild Weather Page
   http://www.wildwildweather.com/twisters.htm
   Find answers to many questions about tornadoes at this site. Be sure to visit the Fujita scale page at http://www.wildwildweather.com/fujita.htm.

Tornado Project Online
   http://www.tornadoproject.com
   This website presents a wealth of tornado information, from myths to safety tips.

Forces of Nature. Directed by George Casey. Washington, DC: National Geographic Society, 2004. DVD.
   This thrilling film shows the overwhelming power of tornadoes and documents the damage they cause.

Nature's Fury. Directed by Jaime Bernanke. Washington, DC: National Geographic Society, 1994. DVD.
   Join tornado hunters on the job, and learn the methods they use to predict where these destructive storms will strike.

Target Tornado: The Science of Storm Chasing. Atlanta: Weather Channel Video, 1996. Videocassette.
   Find out what it's like to chase tornadoes with the Weather Channel.

The Wizard of Oz. Directed by Victor Fleming. Hollywood, CA: Warner Bros. Studios, 1939. DVD.
   This is the classic film of Dorothy, Toto, the Tin Man, the Scarecrow, and the Cowardly Lion, who find themselves together after a tornado carries Dorothy from Kansas to Oz.

Index

Photo Acknowledgments

The photographs in this book are used with the permission of: Marvin Nauman/FEMA, p.1; Courtesy of the National Oceanic and Atmospheric Administration Central Library Photo Collection, pp. 3, 16, 17, 19, 20, 21, 23 (both), 24 (both), 25, 29 (top), 34, 36, 37 (both), 46, 48, 49, 55, 56 (top); © Reuters/CORBIS, pp. 4, 38, 43; © John Sommers II/Reuters/CORBIS, p. 5; © Holger Otto/Reuters/CORBIS, p. 7; © Everett Collection, p. 8 (top); © Bettmann/CORBIS, pp. 8 (bottom), 9, 22, 29 (bottom), 31, 32, 35, 56 (bottom); © Eric Nguyen/Jim Reed Photography/CORBIS, p. 11; Webster County Historical Society, pp. 12, 13 (top); State Historical Society of Missouri, Columbia, p. 13 (bottom); © Jim Reed/CORBIS, p. 14; © Zhangjian-Jiangsu/ImageChina/ZUMA Press, p.15; © Stock4B/CORBIS, p. 18; © Michael Mauney/Time Life Pictures/Getty Images, p. 28; © James Gibbard/Tulsa World/ZUMA Press, p. 33; © David Crenshaw/Tulsa World/ZUMA Press, pp. 39, 51; Michael Rieger/FEMA, p. 41; © Farjana K. Godhuly/AFP/Getty Images, p. 44; © AP/Wide World Photos, p. 45; © NOAA/ZUMA Press, p. 47; © Todd Strand/Independent Picture Service, p. 50; © Stormi Greener/Minneapolis Star Tribune/ZUMA Press, p. 53; © Sam Lund/Independent Picture Service, p. 54; © John G. Zimmerman/Time Life Pictures/Getty Images, p. 57 (top); © Harald Richter/AFP/Getty Images, p. 57 (middle); © Joseph C. Garza/U.S. Navy/Handout/Reuters/CORBIS, p. 57 (bottom). Diagram by Bill Hauser, p. 21.

Front Cover: © Jim Zuckerman/CORBIS; Back Cover: Courtesy of the National Oceanic and Atmospheric Administration Central Library Photo Collection.

About the Authors

Michael Woods is a science and medical journalist in Washington, D.C., who has won many national writing awards. He works in the Washington Bureau of the *Pittsburgh Post-Gazette* and the *Toledo Blade*. Mary B. Woods has been a librarian in the Fairfax County Public School System in Virginia and the Benjamin Franklin International School in Barcelona, Spain. Their other books include the eight-volume Ancient Technology series. Michael and Mary have four children. When not writing, reading, or enjoying their grandchildren, they travel to gather material for future books.